AMERICA

AMERICA

FROM
AMERIGO VESPUCCI
TO THE
LOUISIANA PURCHASE

The Pierpont Morgan Library

1976

PREFACE

THIS BOOK, which is also the record of an exhibition at The Pierpont Morgan Library, 13 May to 31 July 1976, contains descriptions of one hundred and fifty items which are significant reminders of the development of the American nation, from the reports of its first exploration to the original manuscript of the Proclamation of the Louisiana Purchase in 1803. We begin with the only letter of Amerigo Vespucci in America (1476), the first Latin edition of the celebrated "Columbus Letter" (1493), and the earliest known description of the North American mainland—Verrazzano's letter to the King of France (1524); we go on to the only copy of the "first variety" of the first printing of the Bible in the Western World (Eliot's Indian Bible of 1661–1663) and the only copy of the first printed Thanksgiving Proclamation (1789); we end with the announcement of that giant step to the west which more than doubled the size of the new country, the United States of America.

Along the way there are remarkable documents in American history, particularly from the years of the war for independence and the early decades of the Republic: the first printing of the Declaration of Independence and the first printed draft of the Constitution, letters concerning Benedict Arnold's treason and John Paul Jones's celebrated victory in the *Bon Homme Richard*, letters from La Fayette asking Washington for the command of a division and from Cornwallis asking Washington for terms of surrender, and Burgoyne sending the terms for surrender at Saratoga. There is a contemporary manuscript of the Articles of Confederation (1781) and Jefferson's letter to the Speaker of the House of Delegates informing him of the "ratification of the Confederation of the thirteen United States of America," the manuscript of a proclamation against Daniel Shays in his rebellion of 1786–1787, and the manuscript proposal of the Eleventh Amendment to the Constitution (1793). With these there are also simple tales of soldiers, sailors, and farmers—diaries of men in the Revolutionary War, the observations by our first naturalists and scientists, drawings by our earliest artists, music and literature from our Colonial days.

The selection of American manuscripts, books, maps, drawings, and other items of historical interest centers on the year 1776. All of the items described in this volume, except about ten, come from the Morgan Library. As in a number of recent exhibitions, we have added a few works from private collections, most of which have not previously been shown.

The collections of Americana in the Library have rarely been exhibited and are not widely known to scholars, at least in comparison with the principal collections of European, English, and ancient Near Eastern literature, history, and art. But to Junius S. Morgan, Pierpont Morgan, and J. P. Morgan, and in the early days of the Library, American history and literature clearly were absorbing interests. Gradually the focus of collecting became European, and this Library did not compete with other major libraries in the city or in nearby states, where the primary concern might be American.

All of the items from the Morgan Library described in this volume were bought by Pierpont Morgan, his father, or his son, unless otherwise indicated. Each one of these men was immensely proud of the great Americana he owned. In 1877 a considerable number of distinguished Americans gave a dinner at Delmonico's in New York to honor "Junius S. Morgan, Esq., of London." In his reply to a speech given by Governor Tilden, Junius Morgan referred to a long letter in his possession which was written in 1788 by George Washington to a friend in England, Sir Edward Newenham (it is described in this book). Mr. Morgan ended by quoting Washington's prediction that if we "continue United & faithful to ourselves," no power can "prevent us from becoming a great, respectable & a commercial nation."

In the years after 1877, the Morgans collected thousands of manuscripts and books which are crucial to our knowledge of American history. In the Morgan Library there are two sets of Signers of the Declaration of Independence (including the only letter known by Button Gwinnett, and his will, and one of the two letters known by Thomas Lynch, Jr.); a third set was given by Pierpont Morgan to the Library of

Congress in 1912. For the chief figures in Colonial and early Federal history we have selected only a handful or two of the documents in the Morgan Library: for example, you will find described here only three of the over one hundred letters of Washington, only three of the two hundred and forty letters of Jefferson, one of the twenty-three letters of Madison, and just one of the approximately two hundred and fifteen drawings by Benjamin West.

Originally we had planned a much more comprehensive catalogue of our American historical collections, and a larger exhibition. But our inability to get any very strong support from endowments, foundations, or corporations necessitated this briefer book and exhibition. We feel nevertheless that we have been able to present a survey of the first two hundred and fifty years of American history marked by its principal milestones. It also shows some of few remaining records of ordinary men in those early days, and souvenirs which bring back memories of great events (a piece of the Concord Bridge) or of historic figures (two stars from George Washington's uniform or bits of Martha Washington's wedding dress). We have tried to make the years of exploration, of colonization, and of the new Republic come alive with both the grandest and the simplest memorials of the beginnings of this country. We hope that this small book will show that not least of the thousands of treasures in the Morgan Library are many relating to the history of this country and this continent. And there are important holdings after 1803, especially relating to Lincoln and the Civil War, and to the history of the Presidency, down to the present day.

We are deeply grateful to the New York State Bicentennial Commission for a grant of three thousand dollars towards this publication and the exhibition, and to The Charles W. Engelhard Foundation for support of all our publications. We are also happy to announce that we have had for the first time help from several corporations, or their foundations, for the general public programs of the Library: the Morgan Guaranty Trust Company of New York Charitable Trust, the American Metal Climax Foundation, the Bristol-Myers Company, the First National City Bank, and the New York Life Insurance Company. We are also grateful to the New York State Council on the Arts which this year for the first time has contributed to the Library's exhibition program.

The catalogue which follows has been prepared by Mr. Herbert Cahoon, Curator of Autograph Manuscripts in the Library. He has selected the quotations which illustrate many of the entries. We are very much indebted to the lenders to the exhibition; they have been willing to let us show some of the most important American documents in private or public collections. There are two anonymous loans, and others from Mrs. Charles W. Engelhard, Mr. H. Bradley Martin, Mr. and Mrs. Constantine Sidamon-Eristoff, and the Heineman Foundation for Research, Educational, Charitable and Scientific Purposes, Inc. (books and manuscripts from the library of Dannie N. Heineman on deposit in the Morgan Library). Mr. Charles V. Passela and his assistants, Miss Roberta DeGolyer and Mr. Edward Jabbour, Jr., prepared the photographs. Other staff members who have helped in the preparation of the book and the exhibition are Miss Christine Stenstrom, Mr. Thomas V. Lange, and Mr. J. Rigbie Turner. Once again The Stinehour Press and The Meriden Gravure Company have helped us to produce a book which we hope is a worthy memorial of the year of our independence in this two hundredth year of its celebration.

Charles Ryskamp
DIRECTOR

The Early Explorers

[SAINT BRANDON]. *Sand Brandons Buch*. [Augsburg: Anton Sorg, c. 1476]. Saint Brendan of Clonfert, a sixth-century priest whose life was written shortly after the year 900, is one of the most famous of the legendary Irish voyagers to the islands of the Atlantic and perhaps to the American continent itself. He was searching for a Western haven for a group of monks and the woodcut illustrations portray some of his adventures.

[CARADOC OF LLANCARVAN]. *The historie of Cambria*. [London: R. Newberie and H. Denham, 1584]. Sixteenth-century Welsh antiquarians claimed to have discovered the story of the Welsh prince Madoc, who sailed from Britain to lands far westward about 1170, where he founded a colony. The legend grew up in Wales that Britain had priority in the discovery of America, and rumors of Indians descended from the Welsh occurred from time to time during the exploration of Western America. Madoc's name and a sea voyage he made are recorded in a fifteenth-century poem, but nothing more is known. "This Madoc arriving in that Westerne countrie, unto the which he came, in the yeare 1170, left most of his people there: and returning backe for more of his owne nation."

PTOLEMY. *Cosmographia*. Bologna: Dominicus de Lapis, 23 June "1462" [i.e., 1477]. The first illustrated Ptolemy, and hence the first printed atlas. So far as is known, these are the first maps to be printed from copper-plates, several earlier woodcut maps being known. The engravings were done by Taddeo Crivelli, otherwise known as a miniaturist. Although the book is dated in the colophon to 1462 (in Roman numerals), documentary evidence proves that this was a misprint for 1477. The map of the world before the voyages of the early explorers.

HANNS RUST, fl. 1472–1497. *Mappa Mundi.* Augsburg. XV century. The only surviving copy of one of the earliest German world maps. It was probably printed at Augsburg in the third quarter of the fifteenth century, and shows the developed map of the world of the Middle Ages. This map was preserved by being pasted to the inner front cover of a 1472 edition of Strabo's *Geographia.*

AMERIGO VESPUCCI, 1451–1512. Autograph letter in Latin signed "Emericus Vespucius," dated Trebbio di Mugello, 19 October 1476, to his father in Florence. 1 p. Vespucci made five voyages to the New World, the last in 1507. Waldsemüller's book, *Cosmographia Introductio* (1507), first gives the name of "America" to the New World. This is the only recorded letter by Vespucci in an American collection. "Do not wonder that I have not written you within the last few days. For I thought that uncle, on his arrival, would make my excuses; he, being away, I did not dare put your letters in Latin, though I am not at all ashamed to write in my mother tongue."

AMERIGO VESPUCCI, 1451–1512. *Mundus novus.* [N.p., n.d.]. Three Latin translations of Vespucci's account of his third voyage to America (1501–1502) were published in 1504. This is one of two which are undated and it may have been published in Rome or in Paris. The account is written in the form of a letter to Lorenzo di Piero Francesco de' Medici. About seven copies of this undated edition are known.

CHRISTOPHER COLUMBUS, c. 1446–1506. *Epistola de insulis nuper inventis.* [Rome: Stephan Plannck, after 29 April 1493]. The first edition in Latin of the "Columbus Letter," the first printed account of the New World. "All these islands are most beautiful and distinguished by various qualities; one can travel through them, and they are full of a great variety of trees which brush at the stars; and I believe they never lose their foliage."

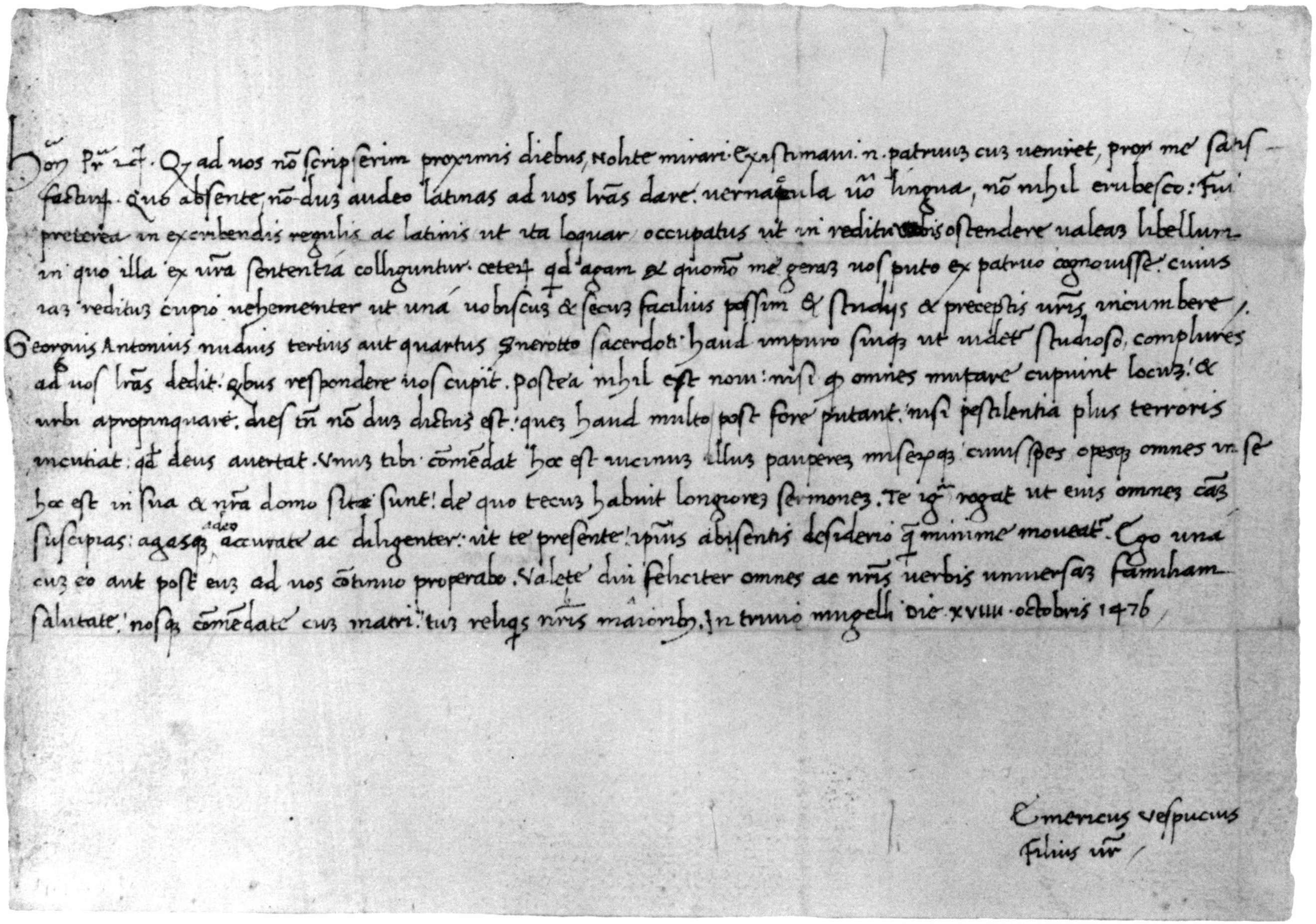
Hon Pr etc. Q ad uos nō scripserim proximis diebus, nolite mirari. Existimaui n. patruum cum ueniret, pro me satis
facturum. Quo absente, nō dum audeo latinas ad uos lrās dare. uernacula uō lingua, nō nihil erubesco. Fui
preterea in excribendis regulis ac latinis ut ita loquar occupatus ut in reditu uris ostendere ualeam libellum
in quo illa ex ura sententia colliguntur. cetera quid agam et quomodo me geram uos puto ex patruo cognouisse. cuius
uram reditum cupio uehementer ut una uobiscum et secum facilius possim et studiis et preceptis uris incumbere /.
Georgius Antonius nuntius tertius aut quartus generotto sacerdoti haud impuro simul ut uidetur studioso, complures
ad uos lrās dedit. quibus respondere uos cupit. postea nihil est noui: nisi quod omnes mutare cupiunt locum. et
urbi apropinquare. dies tn nō dum dictus est: quem haud multo post fore putant. nisi pestilentia plus terroris
incutiat. quod deus auertat. Unum tibi comedat hoc est uicinum illum pauperem miserumque cuius spes opesque omnes in se
hoc est in sua et ura domo sitae sunt: de quo tecum habuit longiores sermones. Te igitur rogat ut eius omnes causas
suscipias: agasque adeo accurate ac diligenter: ut te presente ipsius absentis desiderio quam minime moueat. Ego una
cum eo aut post eum ad uos continuo properabo. Valete diu feliciter omnes ac uris uerbis uniuersam familiam
salutate. nosque comedate cum matri tum reliquis uris maioribus. In triuio mugelli die xviiii octobris 1476 /

Emericus Vespucius
Filius uester /

AMERIGO VESPUCCI Autograph Letter 1476

FRANCANZANO MONTALBODDO. *Newe unbekanthe landte und ein newe weldte.* [Nureinbergk: G. Stüchssen, 1508]. The first collection of voyages printed in German, translated by Jobst Ruckamer, from Montalboddo's compilation, *Paesi novamente retrovati*, first published in Vicenza in 1507. It contains the accounts of three voyages of Columbus and the third voyage of Vespucci. In German translation Columbus becomes Dawber (the dove) and Lorenzo de' Medici becomes Laurentz Artzt (the physician). The unusual title page with scrolls is adapted from the Italian edition.

GIOVANNI DA VERRAZZANO, 1485–1528. [*Del Viaggio del Verazzano Nobile Fiorentino al Servizio di Francesco I. Ri de Francia, fatto nel 1524 all'America Settentrionale*]. 21 p. Verrazzano's account of his voyage along the Atlantic coast of North America in 1524 from the Carolinas to Cape Breton and Newfoundland. This manuscript, known as the Cèllere Codex, is in a scribal hand but has a number of annotations that are believed by scholars to be in Verrazzano's autograph; it is the earliest and most important text of Verrazzano's discoveries and the earliest known account of the North American mainland. On 17 April Verrazzano discovered New York Bay. The men of his ship, the *Dauphine*, were greeted by the surprised and friendly Indians who came to meet them, and who pointed out an easy landing place, probably at the present site of Tompkinsville on Staten Island. From there by small boat they ventured into the Upper Bay, measured its depth, and estimated its size. The land received the name *Angoulême*, the family name of Francis I.

GIOVANNI BATTISTA RAMUSIO, 1485–1557. *Delle navigatione et viaggi . . .* [volume 3]. Venice: Stamperia de' Giunti, 1565. The third part of Ramusio's treatise on navigation and voyages contains the first printing of the first version of Verrazzano's voyage. This version was translated into English by Hakluyt for his *Divers voyages* of 1582.

per lo quale andauamo discorrendo da Luna et Laltra parte al numero di
xxx di loro barchette có ísinite gente che passauano da Luna et Laltra
terra per uederci. i uno stanke come auenir suole nel nauicare, mouen-
dosi uno ípeto diuento cotrario dal mare súmo forzati tornarci ala
naue lassando la detta terra có molto dispiacere, p la comodita ej uaghza
di quella pensando nó fussi senza qualche faculta di prezo, móstradosi
tutti e colli di glla minerali. leuata lancora nauigando iuerso oriente
ch cosi laterra tornaua, discorsi leghe Lxxx sempre a uista di glla
Discoprimo una ísola í forma triangulare, lontana dal cótinete leghe
dietj, di grandeza simile ala ísula di Rhodo piena di colli,
coperta d'albori molto popolata, p có hnoui fuochi per tutto al Lito
intorno uedemmo faceuano. baptizamola in nome de la vra clarissima
genitrice, no surgendo a quell p la opposithone dl tempo. Peruenimo
a una altra terra distante dale ínsula leghe xv, doue trouamo uno
bellissimo porto, p prima che í quello entrassimo uedemo circa di
xx barchette di gente che ueniuano có uary gridi ej marauigle
ítorno ala naue, nó aproximandosi apiu di ciquata passi fermauosi
guardando lhedificio. La nra effigie et habiti, di poi tutti ísieme
spandeuano uno alto grido, significando rallegrarsj. Assicuratilj alquato
imitando loro gesti saproximorono tanto che gittama loro alcunj sonaglj
ej specchi et molte fantasie. le qualj prese có riso riguardandole
sicuramete ne la naue entrorono. Erano ítra quellj duoj Re di
tanta bella statura ej forma quáto narrare sia possibile. El primo di
ánj xxxx l circa. laltro giouane di annj xxiij. l'habito de
qualj tale era. El piu uecchio sopra il corpo nudo haueua una pelle

THE BAILLY GLOBE. This copper globe was constructed in 1530 by Robert de Bailly. It is one of three examples, each signed "Robertus Bailly 1530." Many nineteenth-century skeptics denied the authenticity of Verrazzano's 1524 voyage because they thought that no vestige remained in French written records or in cartographical representation in support of the Verrazzano achievement. This negation was controverted by the Cellere Codex which came to the attention of scholars in 1909 and this Bailly Globe purchased by J. Pierpont Morgan in 1912. The cartographical details of the globe are based on maps drawn in 1529 by Gerolamo da Verrazzano, the explorer's brother. He labels the North American continent "Verrazana."

ANTONIUS SPANO. *Ivory Globe.* 1593. This fine ivory globe was signed and dated by a Calabrian artist, Antonius Spano, with a presentation inscription to the Infante, later King Philip III of Spain. The inscription tells the prince that *totus orbis ad se gubernandum te vocat et expectat*, "the whole world calls to you and awaits your governance"—words which now read ironically in light of the general incompetence of his reign.

NICOLAS MONARDES, c. 1512–1588. *Ioyfull newes out of the new-found worlde.* London: E. Allde, 1596. The third edition of the first American herbal; it was originally published in English in 1577. John Frampton was an English merchant who had been imprisoned by the Spanish Inquisition and who took some pleasure in making the riches of the New World better known to Englishmen of commerce who might break the Spanish monopoly. The author describes the killing of whales in Florida in search of ambergris, "They that come from Florida say, that there bee Whaltes by those coastes, and that they have killed some of them, and founde neyther *Ambar* nor other thing in their Mawes, more then fishes; & also in the yong Whales which are very greate, although they have killed them, that they found nothing in them."

PIERRE DESCELIERS. *Portolan Atlas*. Dieppe?, c. 1545. M. 506. Desceliers, one of the most important early French mapmakers, may have taught nautical science at Dieppe. His maps are both highly decorative and very up-to-date in their geographical information. This atlas relates closely to (but seems to be earlier than) a signed atlas of 1546, now in the John Rylands Library, which Desceliers made for the Dauphin.

BATTISTA AGNESE. *Portolan Atlas*. Venice, c. 1542–1545. M. 460. Agnese was a Genoese cartographer who worked in Venice. He executed a large number of portolan-style (i.e., coastal) atlases, of remarkable beauty, dating roughly between 1536 and 1564. Most of them contain the world map, with lines marking the route of the Magellanic circumnavigation, and the route from Spain to Panama, across the isthmus and on to Peru.

BATTISTA AGNESE. *Portolan Atlas*. Venice, 15 May 1542. M. 507. This atlas of Agnese is signed and dated by him on another of its maps. This map is the earliest known with place names showing knowledge of Francisco de Ulloa's exploration of Baja California in 1539–1540. Yucatan is still represented as an island rather than a peninsula.

THEODORE DE BRY, 1528–1598. [Collection of voyages]. Franckfort am Main, 1590–1628. The de Bry volumes—these are from the Latin edition— are of incomparable value for the history of the exploration and Indian customs of Florida and the West Indies. The Flemish engravers, father and son, based their engravings on the work of Jacob Le Moyne and the English artist John White, among others.

SAMUEL DE CHAMPLAIN, c. 1570–1635. Document signed, dated 22 July 1617. 1 p. One of the few existing autograph signatures of the great explorer, and dated the year following his discovery of Lakes Huron and Ontario. The document, which is also signed by Champlain's wife, Hélène Boullé, is a contract for a servant.

SAMUEL DE CHAMPLAIN, c. 1570–1635. *Voyages et descouvertures faites en la Nouvelle France*. Paris: Claude Collet, 1619. From the standpoint of ethnology, the account of Champlain's expedition of 1615–1616 is by far the most important of the three that he made. Not only did he describe three nations hitherto unknown, but he also spent a winter in the Huron villages—having been forced to do so by a wound received in another battle against the Iroquois. The winter was a most uncomfortable one for him, but he was able to observe the Hurons' daily life from an intimate vantage point.

JOHN SMITH, 1579–1631. *The generall historie of Virginia, New-England and the Summer Isles*. London: Michael Sparkes, 1624. Captain Smith was the leader of the first permanent English colony in America at Jamestown in Virginia and explored the coasts of what is now Maine and Massachusetts. He published a number of books intended to encourage trade and colonization in America; the *Generall historie* is his masterpiece and is the first sizeable work in England about the New World. The engraved map of "Ould Virginia" (fourth state) shows Pocahontas saving the life of Captain Smith. "This plaine History humbly sheweth the truth; that our most royall King James hath place and opportunitie to inlarge his ancient Dominions without wronging any."

American Indians

WILLIAM WOOD, 1580–1639. *New Englands Prospect*. London: Tho. Cotes, 1635. Wood lived in New England for four years and on his return produced this descriptive narrative. The first part is valuable as a topographical guide and the map of "The South part of New-England" is more correct than any previous one. The second part contains very important observations of the Indians of New England and their neighbors. The characteristics and customs of the different tribes are carefully described and there is also a brief Indian vocabulary which takes precedence over the linguistic labors of John Eliot, Roger Williams, and others. "As he that kills a Deere, sends for his friends, and eates it merrily: So he that receives but a piece of bread from an English hand, parts it equally betweene himselfe and his comerades, and eates it lovingly. In a word, a friend can command his friend, his house, and whatsoever is his, (saving his Wife) and have it freely."

Gift of Henry S. Morgan.

THE HOLY BIBLE: CONTAINING THE OLD TESTAMENT AND THE NEW. TRANSLATED INTO THE INDIAN LANGUAGE. Cambridge: Samuel Green and Marmaduke Johnson, 1663–1661. This is the first printing of the Bible in the Western World and also the first complete Bible to be printed in a non-European language for missionary purposes. The translation by John Eliot is in the Massachusetts dialect of the Algonkin family of languages, which was spoken by a large tribe, now extinct. This is the only recorded copy of what is known as the "first variety" of the Indian Bible. It has the English and Indian title pages to both the Old (1663) and New Testaments (1661), and also the dedicatory epistles in English both to the whole Bible and to the New Testament. This copy was presented by John Eliot to Thomas Shepard, minister at Charlestown, in 1666.

THE HOLY BIBLE: CONTAINING THE OLD TESTAMENT AND THE NEW. TRANSLATED INTO THE INDIAN LANGUAGE. Cambridge: Samuel Green and Marmaduke Johnson, 1663–1661. This copy is of the "second variety" of the Bible for it does not have the English title page and dedication to the New Testament. It was once owned by White Kennett, bishop of Peterborough (1660–1728), historian, antiquarian, and an original member of the Society for Propagating the Gospel in Foreign Parts.

MAMUSSE WUNNEETUPANATAMWE UP-BIBLUM GOD NANEESWE NUK-KONE TESTAMENT KAH WONK WUSKU TESTAMENT. Cambridge: Samuel Green, 1685–1680. A second edition of Eliot's Indian Bible was eventually called for, and Eliot was assisted in a new revision by John Cotton, minister of Plymouth. Some errors made in printing and in translating in the first edition are corrected here and would be of value were there anyone to read this ancient language of America. The Library has two copies of this edition, one bound as a single volume, and one with the Old and New Testaments bound separately.

JOHN ELIOT, 1604–1690. *The Indian grammar begun*. Cambridge: Marmaduke Johnson, 1666. The literary fame of the Apostle to the Indians, John Eliot, rests upon his translation of the whole Bible into the Indian language. It is not always remembered that he compiled several other books in his effort to organize the unwritten Indian language and to provide it with rules. This *Indian grammar* is, perhaps, the most important, though not the earliest, of his linguistic studies. "This language doth greatly delight in Compounding of words, for Abbreviation, to speak much in few words, though they be some-times long."

INCREASE MATHER, 1639–1723. *A brief history of the war with the Indians in New-England*. Boston: John Foster, 1676. It is not difficult to see why the relations between the English and the Indians caused so much tragedy for so many years. The English in New England methodically took the Indians' land, and when confronted with opposition reacted with violence. Increase Mather gives a thorough, if one-sided, account of the Indian War of 1675–1676, but reveals no sympathy for the Indians. "That the Heathen People amongst whom we live, and whose Land the Lord God of our Fathers hath given to us for a rightfull Possession, have at sundry times been plotting mischievous devices against that part of the English Israel which is seated in these goings down of the Sun, no man that is an Inhabitant of any considerable standing, can be ignorant."

WILLIAM HUBBARD, 1621–1704. *A narrative of the troubles with the Indians in New-England*. Boston: John Foster, 1677. Hubbard's book appeared after King Philip's War had ended, when the people of New England were still aroused against the Indians. But Hubbard, a clergyman, was fair-minded in his treatment of the Indians. He furnished an account of the Pequod War of 1637, during which most of the members of the Pequod tribe were annihilated. This is a copy of the first edition, first issue, of the book with the White Hills map, the first map engraved and printed in English America. "There are about six Societies of Indians in the Country, who have professedly owned themselves Christians; In every one of which it is supposed there are some, that do make a serious profession of the Christian Religion. The Salvation of whose Souls is worth far more pains and cost than ever yet was laid out upon that work."

MORGAN GODWYN. *The Negro's & Indians Advocate, suing for their admission into the Church*. London: Printed for the Author, by J. D., 1680. Godwyn was a minister in Virginia for several years under the government of Sir William Berkeley; he also spent some time in the West Indies. He was a strong believer in the propagation of the faith. "That the Negro's (both Slaves and others) have naturally an equal Right with other Men, to the Exercise and Privileges of Religion; of which 'tis most unjust in any part to deprive them."

MOHAWK INDIAN DEED. Document signed by eight members of the Mohawk tribes with their marks and seals, dated Schenectady, New York, 13 April 1714. 1 p. The document is a deed of transfer granting to Adam Vrooman of Schenectady two hundred acres of meadowland and sixty acres of woodland. The terms were ". . . for Divers Considerations. But more especially for the Love, favour, and affection which we have and do bear towards Our loving friend and acquaintance, Adam Vrooman, Esq."

THE BOOK OF COMMON PRAYER IN THE MOHAWK LANGUAGE. New-York: William Bradford, 1715. The first edition of the first surviving *Book of Common Prayer* in any language to have been printed in what is now the United States, and a book of great rarity. It is entirely in the Mohawk language except for the English title and the headings to the prayers. The volume was printed by William Bradford, who established the first printing presses in both Philadelphia and New York.

THE ORDER FOR MORNING AND EVENING PRAYER IN THE MOHAWK LANGUAGE. [New York]: Printed in the Year, 1769. This 1769 edition of the *Book of Common Prayer* in the language of the Mohawk Indians contains prayers for rain and for fair weather. The printing of this edition was begun in New York City in 1763 by William Weyman; his death and that of one of the translators delayed the book and it was finally completed in four hundred copies by Hugh Gaine in 1769.

DAVID BRAINERD, 1718–1747. Autograph leaf from his journal, numbered 13–14, concerning his missionary work among the Indians. [N.p., n.d.]. 2 p. Brainerd, who studied at Yale, was a mystic of saintly character, controlled by a sense of God and duty, but very practical in his missionary program. At the time of his early death he was engaged to marry a daughter of Jonathan Ed-

M OHAWK I NDIAN D EED Schenectady, N.Y. 1714

wards; Edwards later published some of his works. "Had an opportunity to discourse with some of the Indians about their souls concerns, and found one young Man that was much concern'd about this spiritual state, who could talk some English and enquired of me what he must do to be sav'd, and added that some endeavour'd to discourage him from embracing Christianity."

SAMUEL PENHALLOW, 1665–1726. *The History of the wars of New-England, with the Eastern Indians.* Boston: T. Fleet, 1726. The best contemporary account of the New England phase of Queen Anne's War and of Lovewell's fight. Penhallow, a wealthy merchant and chief justice, believed the wars with the Indians were a punishment from God for the sins of the Puritans, especially for their not converting the Indians to Christianity. "And in as much as the Divine Providence has placed me near the Seat of Action, where I have had greater Opportunities than many others of remarking the Cruelty and Perfidy of the Indian Enemy, I thought it my Duty to keep a Record thereof."

[CADWALLADER COLDEN], 1688–1776. *The History of the Five Indian Nations depending on the Province of New-York in America.* New-York: William Bradford, 1727. One of ten recorded copies of the first history of the Iroquois Confederation and of the first history printed in New York. Colden had considerable knowledge of and sympathy for the Indians; he was also an ardent Loyalist. "The Five Nations are a poor Barbarous People, under the darkest Ignorance, and yet a bright and noble Genius shines thro' these black Clouds. . . . But what have we Christians done to make them better? Alas! we have reason to be ashamed, that these Infidels, by our Conversation and Neighbourhood, are become worse than they were before they knew us."

THOMAS GAGE, 1721–1787. Autograph letter signed, dated New York, 14 September 1767, addressed to Sir William Johnson. 2 p. The British Commander in Chief in North America writes the Superintendent of Indian Affairs, con-

THE SACRED BUCKSKIN OF THE APACHES

cerning the Cherokees and the Northern Indians, and the animosity of the Cherokees in general: ". . . to prove that those Indians do kill white people and Cherokees indiscriminately, when they come to war against the latter, they have sent the Head Piece and Scalp; Which I send herewith." The head piece and scalp have not survived with the letter.

JOSEPH BRANT, 1742–1807. Autograph letter signed, dated Niagara, 17 December 1802, addressed to James [i.e., John] Wheelock. 1 p. Brant was the Mohawk chief who was the principal leader of the Indian troops fighting for the British during the Revolutionary War. He had been educated at Eleazar Wheelock's Indian College—later to become Dartmouth—and this letter informs the President of Dartmouth that his son Jacob is returning to study. "My Son now returns to be under the care of the President, and I sincerely hope he will pay attention to his studies as will do credit to himself and be a comfort to his parents. The horse that Jacob rides out, I wish to be got in good order after he arrives and sold, as an attentive Scholar, has no time to ride about."

THE SACRED BUCKSKIN OF THE APACHES. This medicine skin was owned by Háshkĕ Nílntĕ and was considered one of the most potent belonging to any of the medicine men. With it are an Apache medicine cap, a fetish, and the pouch for the folded medicine skin. During the lifetime of Háshkĕ Nílntĕ it was impossible for any white man even to look upon this wonderful "medicine." After reaching extreme old age, he was killed, presumably by his wife, from whom this valuable and sacred object was acquired by Edward S. Curtis, author of *The North American Indian*. The first volume of this work (1907) gives an outline of the mythology of the Apache people as it is portrayed on this medicine skin; it is the Apache story of the Creation.

Lent anonymously.

THE COLONIES

SIR MARTIN FROBISHER, c. 1539–1594. Document signed by Frobisher and others, dated London, 2 August 1588. 1 p. The document is a resolution of the Admiralty Council concerning the provisioning of ships in the Firth of Scotland. Frobisher was one of the English merchant venturers who sought gold and a Northwest Passage to the Orient. He was a sailor of great experience and ability, but he had the misfortune to carry home shiploads of fool's gold (iron pyrites) from the New World which brought down on him great public ridicule.

RICHARD HAKLUYT, 1552?–1616. *The third and last volume of the voyages, navigations, traffiques, and discoueries of the English Nation.* London: G. Bishop, R. Newberie, and R. Barker, 1600. In the final volume of his important work Hakluyt includes the account of the voyage to the New World made by Sir Humphrey Gilbert, half-brother of Sir Walter Raleigh. In common with other explorers he was looking for the Northwest Passage; he took possession of Newfoundland and was lost in a storm on his return voyage. "The Frigat was neere cast away, oppressed by waues, yet at that time recouered: and giuing foorth signes of ioy, the Generall sitting abaft with a booke in his hand, cried out unto us in the Hind (so oft as we did approch within hearing) *We are as neere to heauen by sea as by land.* Reiterating the same speech, well beseeming a souldier, resolute in Jesus Christ, as I can certifie he was."

RICHARD HAKLUYT, 1552?–1616. *Virginia richly valued, by the description of the maineland of Florida, her next neighbor.* London: Felix Kyngston, 1609. Hakluyt is the translator into English of this first and best account of the expedition of Hernando de Soto. The identity of the original author, "the gentleman of Elvas," is not known. The book was probably published under the auspices of the Virginia Company. Hakluyt, English clergyman and geographer, collected accounts of travels mainly by Englishmen and edited them for publication. His works are of great value for the early history of the New World. De Soto travelled far beyond the boundaries of present-day Florida and died on the shores of the Mississippi River, which he is credited with discovering.

THOMAS MORTON, c. 1575 – c. 1646. *New English Canaan or New Canaan. Containing an Abstract of New England.* Amsterdam: J. F. Stam, 1637. Morton represented the Anglican and anti-Puritan factions in England and brought his beliefs to the New World. In 1622, with a group of fellow immigrants he set up the colony of Merry Mount, where he set up a maypole for his friends and the Indians to dance around. He was twice deported from Massachusetts Bay, and published this impious account of the Puritans. Morton's accounts of the Indians and natural history are of importance; his satire of the settlers' social life is amusing but probably inaccurate. "And for the water, therein it excelleth Canaan by much; for the Land is so apt for Fountaines, a man cannot digg amisse, therefore if the Abrahams and Lots of our time come thether, there needs be no contention for wells."

[NATHANIEL WARD], c. 1578 – c. 1652. *The simple cobler of Aggawam in America. Willing to help mend his native country, lamentably tattered, both in the upper-leather and sole, with all the honest stitches he can take.* London: John Dever & Robert Ibbitson for Stephen Bowtell, 1647. Ward, who published this book under a pseudonym, was a clergyman in Aggawam (Ipswich), Massachusetts. The book is a satire of England and New England during the quarrel between Parliament and the Crown, of the human race in general, and women in particular, for being silly. With a copy of the second edition published the same year as the first. "The world is full of care, much like unto a bubble; Women and care, and care and women, and women and care and trouble."

PETER STUYVESANT, c. 1610–1672. Document in Dutch, signed, dated Fort Amsterdam, New Netherlands, 1649. 1 p. Stuyvesant was the headstrong and autocratic director general of New Netherlands from 1646 until the surrender of the colony to the English in 1664. In this document, which he has signed once in 1649 and again in 1659, he makes a grant of land to Jan Huygen. Huygen was a religious leader of the colony, and the land defined in this grant is approximately that of the present Nos. 17–19 Broadway.

BESCHRIJVINGHE VAN VIRGINIA, NIEUW NEDERLANDT, NIEUW ENGELANDT. . . . Amsterdam: Joost Hartgers, 1651. This representation of Manhattan about 1626–1628 is, if authentic, the earliest known view. Some historians believe that the view owes its origin to Hartger's fertile imagination, but others point out that the scene, particularly when reversed, becomes so suggestive of reality that it is likely that it actually had some basis in fact.

JOHN ELIOT, 1604–1690. Document signed, dated [Boston, Massachusetts] 25 August 1655. 2 p. This decision of the General Court, signed by Eliot, Richard Mather, James Mason, and others, concerns the support of the son of Joseph and Susan Heiden, physically and mentally disturbed by the "distemper." It orders that the parents be provided for during the lamentable condition of their son "for the preventing of Great Evill, and for their support under that burden wch (being so lowe as they are) is unsupportable upon them, however tenderly affected towards their own child."
Gift of DeCoursey Fales.

WILLIAM PENN, 1644–1718. Autograph letter signed, dated Philadelphia, 6 June 1684, addressed to his wife in England. 5 p. With this affectionate letter the founder of Pennsylvania enclosed a copy of his last will and testament. He told her of his imminent departure for England and wrote, "My most dear

G[ulielma] Penn. Being now to leave this part of the world and ready to come to you not knowing how the lord pleaseth to deal with me in my passage, least the sea be my grave, and the deeps my sepulchre, I write unto thee as my beloved one, the true and great joy and crown of my life above all visible comforts, allways valued by me and honored above women; I do most dearly salute and embrace thee with thy dear children praying the god of our many and rich blessings to be with you and that he would preserve you from the evill that is in the world, and among thos that profess a faith that is above it. . . ."

[THOMAS ASH]. *Carolina; or a description of the present state of that country*. London: Printed for W. C., 1682. The earliest account of the Port Royal settlement, written in the spirit of a promotional tract. There is an early mention of corn whiskey. "By Maceration, when duly fermented, a strong Spirit like Brandy may be drawn off from it [the corn], by the help of an Alembick."

JOHN TULLEY, 1638–1701. *An Almanack for the year of our Lord MDCXCII*. Cambridge: S. Green & B. Green, 1692. One of three recorded copies of this year of the almanac, and one which belonged to the Reverend James Pierpont (1659–1714), minister at New Haven, and an ancestor of Pierpont Morgan. The almanac has been interleaved and has a number of diary entries by Pierpont. In October he had to "lay Mrs. Falconer undr Admonition for her scandal of Drunkeness while att Newark." She later made "a very satisfactory & acceptable confession."

REBECKA EAMES. "The humble Petition of Rebecka Eames unto his Excellency Sir Wm. Phipps knight & Governor of their Majestyes Dominions in America humbly sheweth. From Salem prison December ye 5th 1692." On 19 August Rebecka Eames had confessed herself a witch, was tried, convicted, and sentenced to be hanged. She writes, "I know not what I said or did. Your

poor and humble petitioner do beg and implore of your Excellency to grant
me a pardon of my life, not deserving death by man for Witchcraft or any
other sin, that my innocent blood may not be shed.''

ELIZUR KEYSAR. Autograph deposition made to a jury of inquest, sworn to
upon oath at Salem, Massachusetts, on 31 August 1692, giving his reasons for
having accused the Reverend George Burroughs of witchcraft. 1 p. Burroughs
had been executed as a wizard twelve days before this document was written.
"Burroughs did steadfastly fix his eyes upon mee, the same evening being in
my own house in a roome without any light I did see very strange things
appear in ye chimney.''

TO ALL WHOM THESE PRESENTS MAY CONCERN. [New-York: William
Bradford, 1713]. This rare tract deals with early ingratitude of the American
people to their sovereign, Queen Anne. The anonymous author takes the side
of the British government against the rising temper of the Colonials. "Had I
not been an Eye and Ear-Witness of the late rash Measures in this Province, I
could not have believ'd that . . . a Body of People so distinguish'd by many
Marks of Her Majesty's Grace and Favour, could be so ungrateful, as to brand
Her most just and gentle Reign with the odious Name of Tyranny.''

MICHAEL WIGGLESWORTH, 1631–1705. *Meat out of the eater: or, medita-
tions concerning the necessity, end, and usefulness of afflictions unto God's
children.* The fifth edition. Boston: J. Allen for Robert Starke, 1717. Wigglesworth, theologian and physician, was a generous and humble man, beloved
by his congregation. The two books of poetry that he wrote were immensely
popular, but are not readable today. *The Day of Doom* (1662), which outlines
vividly the Puritan doctrines of predestination, original sin, and eternal punishment, was followed in 1669 by *Meat out of the eater*, which is lugubrious,
monotonous, and in very small print. Early editions of both works are very
rare and some have not survived; this is one of two known copies of the fifth

edition of *Meat of the eater* with this imprint. "This world's the vale of Tears; We must not look to be, Whilst we are cloath'd with sinful flesh, From griefs and sorrows free."

COTTON MATHER, 1663–1728. Autograph letter signed, dated Boston, 10 December 1717, addressed to Sir William Ashurst. 2 p. Mather, the greatest intellectual of his time and also the most nauseous personality, comments on the peaceable times enjoyed by New England under "one of the Best of Governours," Samuel Shute. Shute's selection was apparently due to the influence of Ashurst, who took a great interest in New England affairs. Mather also sends "a few of our many & latest publications," and tells of recent deaths of officials of the Colony. "We are Dying! may we be so happy as to finish well, and be preserved faultless by our Great Saviour in the presence of God with exceeding Joy."
Purchased as the gift of P. Angus Morgan.

JAMES RIVINGTON, 1724–1802. Autograph letter signed, dated New York, 16 May 1768, addressed to Samuel Galloway in Annapolis. 1 p. High living and free spending characterized James Rivington, bookseller, printer, and proprietor of *Rivington's New-York Gazetteer*. He came to New York from England in 1760 and at the time this letter was written his bookshops were on the verge of bankruptcy. Rivington was a fine editor and publisher and although he was of Loyalist sympathies is reported to have assisted spies of General Washington during the latter days of the Revolution. In this letter he is concerned with a sick or injured horse and the chances of him racing again.

THOMAS JEFFERYS, d. 1771. *A general topography of North America and the West Indies*. London: Robert Sayer and Thomas Jefferys, 1768. Jefferys was a leading map engraver and also geographer to the Prince of Wales, afterwards George III. This copy of what is popularly known as "Jefferys' Atlas" was owned by George Washington and the maps are numbered in his hand.

RELIGION

ROGER WILLIAMS, c. 1603–1683. *The bloudy tenent, of persecution, for cause of conscience, discussed, in a conference betweene truth and peace.* [London]: Printed, 1644. Williams was a highly educated man of deep religious and civic feeling. In 1635 the Massachusetts General Court sent him to exile in Rhode Island where, with his followers, he founded the city of Providence. He was the first to welcome Jews to any American colony. *The bloudy tenent* is directed against John Cotton, the Boston minister who once denounced democracy as "the meanest and worst of all forms of government." Williams argues that magistrates have no right to interfere in church government, and the clergy have no right to meddle with the magistracy. "I judge it not unfit to give alarme to my selfe, and all men to prepare to be persecuted or hunted for cause of conscience."

THE SPEEDWELL PASSENGER LIST. A Lyst of the Pasingers abord the Speedwell of London Robert Look Master bound for New England. Manuscript. Gravesend, 30 May 1656. The first Quakers to arrive in New England are indicated on the list by a "Q" at the left of the name; there are eight in number. The *Speedwell* landed safely in Boston on 27 June 1656 as is attested by a note in the autograph of Assistant Governor John Endecott of the Massachusetts Bay Colony and signed with his initials.

GUALTHERUS DU BOIS. *Kort-begryp der waare Christelyke leere.* Amsterdam: for Jacobus Goelet in New York, [1706]. This edition of the Heidelberg Catechism was printed for the Dutch-speaking populace of New York under the supervision of Du Bois, who was a pastor in the Dutch Reformed Church here. A Dutch edition of *The Primer of Bible truths* by Jakob Borstius, for the use of children, is added at the end. One of two copies recorded in the United States.

Purchased on the Harper Fund.

GEORGE KEITH, c. 1638–1716. *A journal of travels from New-Hampshire to Caratuck, on the continent of North-America.* London: J. Downing, 1706. Keith, a Scottish-born clergyman and Quaker leader, had a serious difference of opinion with William Penn and founded a splinter group of Quakers who eventually turned to the Church of England. He travelled extensively, especially in the middle Colonies (Caratuck is in North Carolina), preaching against the Quakers, and was a considerable spiritual force. "And I shewed, that the Ministers and People of the Church of England, had a better Belief, Trust, and Hope of the inward Assistances of the Holy Spirit, than the Quakers had, notwithstanding the Quakers proud and presumptuous Affirmations and Pretensions to the Spirit above others."

EDMUND GIBSON, 1669–1748. A Memorial concerning the sending of Bishops to the English Plantations abroad. Manuscript partly autograph and partly secretarial. 22 leaves. This manuscript of the Bishop of London is accompanied by twelve printed forms containing queries to be answered by ministers of various churches in the Colonies. These have been answered by the ministers in considerable detail; of particular interest are the answers to questions about public schools for youth and parochial libraries. Most of the answers are dated in 1724. The Reverend George Ross of New Castle, Pennsylvania (now Delaware), answers the question "Have you a Parochial Library?" with "Yes and the books I perserve in the same good condition, that I do my own."

BIBLIA, DAS IST: DIE HEILIGE SCHRIFT. Germantown: Christoph Saur, 1743. The first Bible in a European language to be printed in what is now the United States. This Luther Bible was produced, the preface tells us, "because so many poor Germans come to this country who do not bring Bibles with them." The edition consisted of 1200 copies, priced at eighteen shillings each. This Bible was reprinted in 1763 and 1776; the printing of the latter edition was interrupted by the Revolution and most sheets were destroyed.

JONATHAN EDWARDS, 1703–1758. Autograph letter signed, dated Stockbridge, 6 August 1753, addressed to the Reverend Joseph Bellamy. 1 p. The famous philosopher, theologian, and missionary has "sent a couple of men for my sheep" and will arrange payment for them after their delivery.

THE HOLY BIBLE. Philadelphia: R. Aitken, 1782. The first complete Bible in English to be published in America. It received an official endorsement by Congress on 12 September 1782. The New Testament, bound separately, is dated 1781.

THE A, B, C. WITH THE CHURCH OF ENGLAND CATECHISM. Philadelphia: Young, Stewart, and M'Culloch, 1785. This pamphlet has been called the "Number One Liturgical Work" in the history of the Protestant Episcopal Church in the United States. It is the first portion of the liturgy from the *Book of Common Prayer* to be published in the new Republic, expressly for the Protestant Episcopal Church. In the text where, according to British practice, one would "honour and obey the King . . . ," the printer has left blanks in place of the references to royalty; he states that "as that form of Expression does not suit our Republican Governments, the Teacher will be pleased to fill up the Blanks with what Words he may deem Expedient."
Purchased on the Acquisitions Fund.

JOHN HANCOCK, 1737–1793. "Thanksgiving Discourse, November 1782." Autograph manuscript unsigned. 20 p. Governor Hancock's discourse is, quite naturally, on the success of the American War. "We are invited to render our solemn Thanks this day to the Supreme Governor of the World, for the Success with which he hath crowned our Arms and those of our Allies; that he hath been a Shield to our Troops in ye Hour of Danger; that he hath in the Year we are closing, more than once led them in Triumph over the Bulwarks of the Foe."

GEORGE WASHINGTON, 1732–1799. *By the President of the United States of America. A Proclamation.* New-York, 1789. The first Thanksgiving proclamation issued at the request of Congress by President Washington on 3 October 1789. Washington named Thursday, 26 November, as the first National Thanksgiving Day. This is the only known copy of the printed proclamation. On that day, Washington noted in his diary: "Being the day appointed for a thanksgiving, I went to St. Paul's Chapel, though it was most inclement and stormy—but few people at Church." Congress requested Washington "To recommend to the People of the United States, a Day of public Thanksgiving and Prayer, to be observed by acknowledging with grateful Hearts the many and signal Favors of Almighty GOD, especially by affording them an Opportunity peaceably to establish a Form of Government for their Safety and Happiness."

FLORA AND FAUNA

JACQUES LE MOYNE DE MORGUES, c. 1533–1588. Sketchbook of studies from nature attributed to Le Moyne. Twenty-nine drawings on sixty-eight leaves. Tempera with some silver and gold wash over faint indications in black chalk. Le Moyne visited Florida in 1564 and made many drawings of flora and fauna and also portraits of Indians. The subjects in this volume include flowers, insects, and small animals, some of which are known in both the Old and New Worlds.

Purchased as the gift of Henry S. Morgan, Mr. and Mrs. William S. Paley, Mr. and Mrs. Richard Salomon, and Mrs. Anne Stern.

MARK CATESBY, 1682–1749. *The natural history of Carolina, Florida and the Bahama Islands.* London: the Author, 1731–1743. Two volumes. This copy of Catesby's great work was once owned by the English naturalist Thomas Pennant. Catesby visited the American Colonies and made many drawings and observations here. The general accuracy of the descriptions, which are in both English and French, and the beauty of the plates made *The natural history* a work of importance, and it went through two more editions before the end of the century.

With an original gouache drawing for the "Kalmia," a type of laurel, which appears in part two of *The natural history of Carolina.* This is one of eight drawings by or attributed to Catesby in the Library's collections.

Gift of Henry S. Morgan.

MARK CATESBY, 1682–1749. Autograph manuscript unsigned and undated, in English, of eleven pages of the Appendix to volume two of his *The natural history of Carolina*, 1743. With some corrections and additions.

Gift of Henry S. Morgan.

GEORGE EDWARDS, 1694–1773. Autograph letter signed, dated London, 5 December 1761, addressed to Thomas Pennant. 2 p. Edwards writes about his fellow naturalist Mark Catesby and discusses topics of natural history. Of Catesby's death he writes, "I beleive he was turnd of 70 when he dyed, whither his death was natural or acidental it is hard to determin, in Crossing the way in holbore he fell and was taken up senceless and so continued 2 or 3 days when he dyed."

Gift of Henry S. Morgan.

GEORGE EDWARDS, 1694–1773. *A natural history of uncommon birds.* London: The Author, [1743]–1751. 4 volumes. *Gleanings of natural history.* London, The Author, 1758–1764. 3 volumes. These volumes contain over two hundred and fifty colored plates of birds, animals, and insects, many of them from the New World. Edwards worked only in England and on the Continent, but corresponded with Linnaeus, Catesby, and other naturalists, and their cooperation is generously acknowledged in his text. As Librarian of the Royal College of Physicians, he received specimens of birds and animals from all over the world. Edwards' rapturous apostrophe to the Creator in his preface to the work on birds has caused it to be said that the book is dedicated to God.

Gift of Mrs. Edward F. Hutton.

GEORGE EDWARDS, 1694–1773. Woodcock. Tempera over faint indications in graphite. This drawing is inscribed in pen on the verso: "Woodcock by George."

Gift of Peter Josten.

JOHN BARTRAM, 1699–1777. *Observations on the inhabitants, climate, soil, rivers, productions, animals, and other matters worthy of notice. Made by Mr. John Bartram, in his travels from Pensilvania to Onondago, Oswego and the Lake Ontario, in Canada. . . .* London: J. Whiston and B. White, 1751. The first American botanist, accompanied by Lewis Evans, the mapmaker, and Conrad Weizer, the Indian scout, made the friendly excursion through Iroquois country that is described in this book. They were later joined by Peter Kalm, the Swedish explorer, who contributed an account of the cataracts at Niagara. "An Englishman when very drunk will fall fast asleep for the most part, but an Indian, when merry, falls to dancing, running, and shouting, which violent action probably may disperse the fumes of the liquor, that had he sat still or remained quiet, might have made him drowsy."

GEORG DIONYS EHRET, 1708–1770. Collection of sixteen water-color drawings on vellum of flowers and fruits, all but one signed, dated 1756–1767. Six of the drawings are of American subjects.

Gift of Junius S. Morgan and Henry S. Morgan.

PIERRE JOSEPH BUC'HOZ, 1731–1807. *Herbier colorié de l'Amérique.* Paris: Chez l'Auteur, 1783. This Alsatian artist and writer produced a large number of books devoted to the flora and fauna of Europe; this is his only book devoted to the plants of America, where he does not seem to have visited. The plates are of high quality and some of them were also published in the author's *Le Jardin d'Eden* (1783–1784).

THE ARTS AND SCIENCES

THE NEW-ENGLAND PRIMER ENLARGED. Boston: T. and J. Fleet, 1763. Over four hundred and fifty issues of the *New-England Primer* were published before 1830; the earliest surviving copy is dated 1727, but the book was probably printed as early as 1686. For well over a century, in its numerous editions, it remained a cornerstone of the education of young Colonials and future Americans. "Thy Life to mend, This Book attend." "My Book and Heart Shall never part."

THE BRITISH INSTRUCTOR: OR THE FIRST BOOK FOR CHILDREN. London: J. and W. Oliver, 1763. The first and only edition of this spelling book for children compiled for use in the Colonies. One of four recorded copies. The anonymous compiler writes in the Preface that "He hath been employed, with renewed pleasure, for several years past in procuring from his friends Bibles, Testaments, and other good books, for the use of the poor Negroes and others abroad, especially in Virginia and South Carolina, and his attempts have been every way attended with remarkable success."

Purchased on the Harper Fund.

PHYLLIS WHEATLEY, C. 1753–1784. *Poems on various subjects, religious and moral.* London: A. Bell, 1773. Phyllis Wheatley was the first distinguished black poet in America. She was educated by a Boston family, the Wheatleys, who recognized her great gifts. She gained fame in England and America for her poems, which owed much to Pope and the neoclassical tradition, and rarely refer to her own lot or life as a slave. "Great God, what light'ning flashes from thine eyes? What pow'r withstands if thou indignant rise?"

Lent by Mr. and Mrs. Constantine Sidamon-Eristoff.

JOHN PAUL JONES, 1747–1792. Autograph letter signed, dated only "Friday" from the *Ranger*, addressed to Hector McNeill, concerning the poet Phyllis Wheatley. 1 p. ". . . pray be so good as put the Inclosed into the hands of the Celebrated Phillis the African Favorite of the Muse and of Apollo—should she Reply—Hope you will be the bearer."

JOHN TRUMBULL, 1750–1831. *M'Fingal: a modern epic poem, in four cantos.* Hartford: Hudson and Goodwin, 1782. The first part of this burlesque satire on the Loyalists appeared in 1775; this is a copy of the first completed edition. M'Fingal is a blundering Loyalist whose arguments prove the opposite case, and he is eventually tarred and feathered. It was a very popular poem during and after the Revolution and there were many printed editions. Trumbull later became a staunch Federalist and a leader of the Hartford Wits.

> "No man e'er felt the halter draw,
> With good opinion of the law;
> Or held in method orthodox
> His love of justice in the stocks."

Purchased on the Harper Fund.

THE LADY'S MAGAZINE AND REPOSITORY OF ENTERTAINING KNOWL-EDGE. Philadelphia: W. Gibbons, 1792. Volume I. This magazine, "submitted with all deference, to the perusal of the fair daughters of Columbia," lasted less than a year. It was one of the earliest American periodicals for women readers and gave as its purpose "to present the Ladies with the most lively prose, and pathetic verse." This volume bears the signature on the title page of William Gedney Tracy (1768–1830), grandfather of the second Mrs. J. Pierpont Morgan.

Gift of Mrs. Paul G. Pennoyer.

PSALMS OF DAVID FOR THE USE OF THE REFORMED DUTCH CHURCH IN NORTH AMERICA. New-York: 1792. A graceful American binding of red morocco with green title-label. The interesting tool of battle emblems used repetitively on the spine seems inappropriate to the text, but the binder probably did not have a large stock of tools to choose from. The influence of contemporary Scottish binding is apparent in the decoration.

Gift of Miss Julia P. Wightman.

[THOMAS DOBSON]. *First lessons for children*. Philadelphia: T. Dobson, 1797. The printer of this American primer was also its author. This copy, one of a very few that are recorded, is in remarkable condition, some of its leaves still being unopened. There are colored woodcuts within the folded leaves as well as without, indicating that the coloring was done by the printer before the book's sheets were folded and stitched and not by a later owner. An extremely early example of an American children's book issued with colored illustrations. "Ducks swim and fly; wild ducks catch fish. Eagles kill little Birds and eat them."

Gift of Charles Ryskamp in honor of Miss Elisabeth Ball.

BENJAMIN WEST, 1738–1820. Rebecca at the well. Point of brush, black wash over black chalk on light-brown paper, some passages outlined in pen and black ink. Inscribed by the artist, "One of the first attempts at historical composition by Benjn West, while in Philadelphia 1757." One of the earliest surviving finished drawings by an American artist.

Purchased as the gift of Mrs. Robert H. Charles.

RAPHAEL LAMAR WEST, 1766–1850. View of the town of Geneva on Seneca

Lake. Pen and ink drawing by the son of Benjamin West during a visit to America which began in 1798.

Purchased as the gift of Mrs. Robert H. Charles.

JOHN SINGLETON COPLEY, 1737–1815. Two studies of a man astride a cannon. Black and white chalk on blue paper. A preparatory drawing for his "The Siege of Gibraltar," which is in the Guildhall Art Gallery, London.

Gift of Mrs. Jacob M. Kaplan.

JOHN DEE, 1527–1608. Letter signed, in Latin, dated Mortlake, 16 January 1577, addressed to Abraham Ortelius in Antwerp. 2 p. Dee was a brilliant mathematician and scholar; no intellectual did so much for English discovery. He was a friend of explorers and scientists in England and in Europe and is said to have coined the phrase "British Empire." In this letter to the great Flemish geographer he asks for details of the North Atlantic, with mentions of the voyages of Frobisher, and of Humphrey Lloyd and Daniel Rogers.

ABRAHAM ORTELIUS, 1527–1598. Autograph letter, in Latin, signed, dated Antwerp, 19 January 1587, addressed to his nephew, Jacob Cole, in London. 2 p. He thanks him for his aid in finding the site of "Wigandecua," which Cole had marked on a map for him as Virginia. "Wigandecua" does not survive as an American place name, but the work of Ortelius as geographer and mapmaker, especially his *Theatrum Orbis Terrarum* (1570), long remained the basis for geographic works.

PLANISPHERIC ASTROLABE FOR USE IN NAVIGATION. Dated 1624, corrected for 1650. Proper use of the astrolabe at sea will find the ship's latitude and give the time of day. William Janszoon Blaeu of Amsterdam was one of the four prominent map and chart makers who flourished in The Netherlands in the seventeenth century; he made this astrolabe. On the last two pages are: (*left*) the Particular Astrolabe with the Rete, or Star Map. This is a circular map of stars, designed in fretwork showing the position of the stars, relatively to one another; lying below the Rete is a plate engraved with circles. (*Right*): the Heavenly Planisphere, which names and gives the position of many of the stars and the twelve signs of the Zodiac.

JOHN JOSSELYN, c. 1630–1675. *New-Englands rarities discovered*. London: G. Widdowes, 1672. The first edition of the first book on the natural history of New England. "The Pond Frog, which chirp in the Spring like Sparrows, and croke like Toads in Autumn: Some of these when they set upon their breech are a Foot high; the Indians will tell you, that up in the Country there are Pond Frogs as big as a Child of a year old."

[BENJAMIN FRANKLIN], 1706–1790. *An account of the new invented Pennsylvanian fire-places*. Philadelphia: B. Franklin, 1744. The resourceful Franklin invented this fireplace to keep his family warmer at less cost. It attracted much attention and this pamphlet was prepared to describe its merits and availability for purchase. The folding plate is an early production of the American geographer Lewis Evans. Only replicas of the fireplace are known to survive, but the original of this pamphlet survives in about twenty copies.

Gift of Henry S. Morgan.

BENJAMIN FRANKLIN, 1706–1790. *Expériences et observations sur l'electricité*. Paris: Durand, 1752. The results of Franklin's experiments, which proved lightning was electricity, were published in London in 1751. They were immediately translated into French and published the following year. The book attracted the attention of King Louis XV, who witnessed some of the experiments as performed by French scientists; he commended Franklin to the

Royal Society in London. This is the King's own, and sumptuously bound, copy.

Lent by the Heineman Collection.

BENJAMIN FRANKLIN, 1706–1790. *L'Armonica. Lettera del signor Beniamino Franklin al padre Giambatista Beccaria.* . . . [Nella reale stamperia di Torino], 1769. Franklin's exposition and elaboration of a new musical instrument here called the "Armonica," but more commonly known as "musical glasses." The letter from Franklin to Beccaria was written in 1762 and tells of his improvements on this instrument already being played in public in England. The text of a cantata by Metastasio, set to music by J. A. Hasse, was performed with the accompaniment of the "Armonica" at a royal wedding in 1769 and prompted the translation and publication of Franklin's letter with Metastasio's poem. This is one of seven recorded copies of the work.

Purchased for the Mary Flagler Cary Music Collection.

GEORGE WASHINGTON, 1732–1799. Autograph surveys signed with drawings in map form, dated in November 1749. These are examples of land surveys made by Washington as a young man in the Western part of Virginia.

Gift of the estate of Hall Park McCullough.

ROBERT ERSKINE, 1735–1780. A map of part of the states of New York and New Jersey: laid down, chiefly from actual surveys, received from the Right Honble. Ld. Stirling & others, and deliniated for the use of His Excely. Genl. Washington by Robert Erskine, F.R.S. 1777. The autograph manuscript signed of one of the most important maps of the American Revolution.

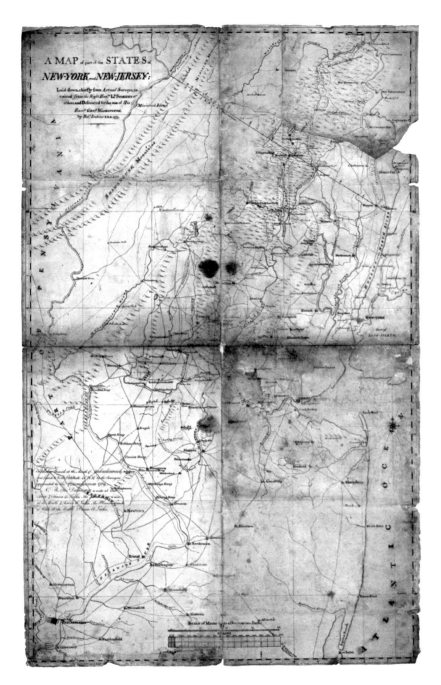

Robert Erskine   Map of Parts of New York and New Jersey   1777

JOHN MORGAN, 1735–1789. Autograph letter signed, dated Philadelphia, 15 July 1765, addressed to Sir Alexander Dick, President of the College of Physicians, near Edinburgh. 3 p. After extensive medical studies abroad, Dr. Morgan returned to his native Philadelphia with the plan for establishing a medical school at the College of Philadelphia. His plan was successful and in this letter he mentions his Commencement oration, *A Discourse upon the Institution of Medical Schools in America*, which has become a medical classic, delivered at the opening of the College of Pennsylvania Medical School in 1765. "Just now I am committing to the Press my inaugural Oration at the College of Philadelphia, in which I have endeavoured to do all the Honour in my Power to Edinburgh." Dr. Morgan later served as medical director of the Continental Army, but was relieved of his office by Congress without any specific charges being brought against him.

Fellows Fund.

ROBERT FULTON, 1765–1815. *A treatise on the improvement of canal navigation.* London: J. and J. Taylor, 1796. After a successful career as an artist, including study in London with Benjamin West, Fulton turned his attention to various aspects of engineering and inventions. The *Treatise*, profusely illustrated by himself, was a prophetic discourse on the economic and political importance of inland waterways. This copy was presented by Fulton to General Kosciusko in 1797; later Thomas Jefferson received it as a gift from the General. With the autograph manuscript of Fulton's "Thoughts on the Delaware and Raritan Canal Act," and a brush and wash drawing of the canal. This canal was completed in 1834 and for a time was an important waterway.

Statesmen

Aaron Burr, 1756–1836. Autograph letter signed, dated Eliz[abeth]town, 2 May 1770, addressed to his sister, Sally. 1 p. Written by the future Vice-President at the age of fourteen. ". . . though I cannot have the Pleasure of seeing you this summer I have nothing more to say at Present but desire to be remembered to Mr. & Mrs. Burr and to all my other Relations."

Patrick Henry, 1736–1799. Letter signed, dated Williamsburgh, 29 June 1776, addressed "To the honourable the President and House of Convention" of Virginia. 2 p. The noted patriot was elected Governor under the new Virginia Constitution of 1776. After being informed of his election he sent this letter of acceptance to the legislature, pledging his services and denouncing British tyranny. Of the Constitution he writes that he hopes ". . . to give permanency and success to that System of Government which you have formed, and which is so wisely calculated to secure equal liberty, and advance human happiness."

Button Gwinnett, 1735–1777. Autograph letter signed, dated 5 May 1773, addressed to Jno. Houston, concerning "Mrs. Stevens' Demand." 1 p. This brief note is the only known letter in the hand of Gwinnett, one of the signers of the Declaration of Independence from Georgia. The Morgan Library has two complete sets of letters and documents written and signed by the Signers of the Declaration of Independence.

Button Gwinnett, 1735–1777. Autograph last will and testament, dated

Savannah March 15th 1777

I'm sound in Body and Mind for which I am under
the highest obligations to the Supreme Being, How
long I shall remain so God only knoweth; I there-
-fore Dispose of my Property both real & Personal
in the Following manner —

First Let all my Just Debts be Discharged then
One half of my Real and Personal Estate remain-
-ing be divided between my Wife and Daughter
in equal Shares —

The other Half of my Estate both real & Personal
shall belong to and Appertain unto the Rev.d
Mr Tho.s Bosomworth his Heirs and Assigns for
ever he the said Tho.s Bosomworth first giving a
rec.t in full of all other Demands —

This is my last Will and Testament and I hereby
revoke all other wills and Codicils —

The above is only intended to convey my Estate in
America

I hereby appoint Tho.s Savage and Lyman Hall Esq.rs
as Executors to this my last Will and Testament

Witness

Jas Joly
W.m Horsby
Thos Bosomworth

Button Gwinnett

BUTTON GWINNETT   Autograph Last Will and Testament   1777

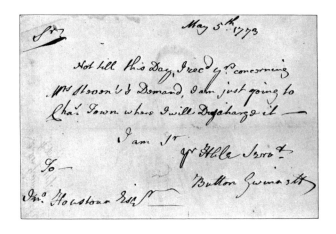

Button Gwinnett   Autograph Letter Signed   1773

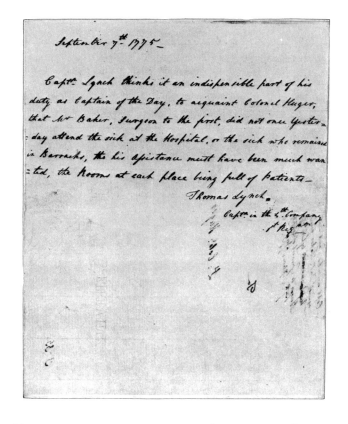

Thomas Lynch, Jr.   Autograph Letter Signed   1775

Savannah, 15 March 1777. 1 p. Only two months later, Gwinnett was fatally wounded in a duel with General Lachlan McIntosh.

THOMAS LYNCH, JR., 1749–1779. Autograph letter signed, dated 7 September 1775, addressed to Lt. Col. Huger. 1 p. One of two surviving letters written by this Signer of the Declaration of Independence. "Captn Lynch thinks it an indispensible part of his duty as Captain of the Day, to acquaint Colonel Huger, that Mr. Baker, Surgeon to the first, did not once yesterday attend the sick at the Hospital, or the sick who remained in Barracks, tho his assistance must have been much wanted, the Room at each place being full of Patients."

THE ARTICLES OF CONFEDERATION. Contemporary manuscript in a secretarial hand. [N.p., 1781]. 7 p. The Articles of Confederation were the law of the United States for eight years (March 1781 – March 1789). It was a faulty document in many ways, for it gave too much power to the States and did not provide for a Federal executive and judiciary. But these Articles served well as a stepping-stone to the Constitution of 1789; without them a system of confederation after Yorktown would have been difficult to secure.

THOMAS JEFFERSON, 1743–1826. Autograph letter signed, dated "In Council," 17 March 1781, addressed to Richard Henry Lee, Speaker of the House of Delegates. 1 p. Governor Jefferson writes, "The inclosed Act of Congress will inform you of the final ratification of the Confederation of the thirteen United States of America. I beg leave to congratulate the General Assembly on this very important event, by which a firm bond of Union is drawn of these states, our friends enabled to repose confidence in our engagements, and our enemies deprived of their only remaining hope."

GEORGE WASHINGTON, 1732–1799. Washington relics. Hair from the head of General and Mrs. Washington and two stars from his uniform.

MARTHA WASHINGTON, 1732–1802. Three pieces of cloth and two pieces of lace from Martha Washington's wedding dress when she married George Washington at St. Peter's Church, New Kent County, Virginia, 5 October 1759. The pieces, received from two different sources, match.

MARY BALL WASHINGTON, 1708–1789. Autograph letter signed, dated 13 March 1782, addressed to her son, George. 1 p. Letters in the hand of the mother of the first President are exceedingly rare. This one has suffered considerable damage by burning, it is said, in the fire that destroyed much of the city of Washington in 1814. "My Not being at home when you went throu fredirecksburg it was a unlucky thing for me now I am afraid I Never shall have that pleasure agin. I am soe very unwell & this trip over the Mountains has almost killd me."

GEORGE WASHINGTON, 1732–1799. Autograph letter signed, dated Mount Vernon, 29 August 1788, addressed to Sir Edward Newenham, the Irish statesman. 6 p. This important letter was owned in 1877 by Junius S. Morgan, father of J. Pierpont Morgan. "I hope the United States of America will be able to keep disengaged from the labyrinth of European politics & Wars; . . . And it is not in the ability of the proudest and most potent people on earth to prevent us from becoming a great, a respectable & a commercial nation, if we shall continue United & faithful to ourselves."

THOMAS PAINE, 1737–1809. Autograph letter signed, dated London, 13

February 1792, addressed to President Washington. 1 p. Paine forwards copies of the second part of his *Rights of Man* to President Washington, to whom the work was dedicated. In this second part Paine called for an overthrow of the British monarchy and hoped it would have the same influence that *Common Sense* had in America. Instead, Paine had to flee to France. "I have had a Doz Copies of my new work put up for the purpose (the work being not yet published) to present to you and Mr. Jefferson. I hope the fifty Copies which were sent to Portsmouth (England) to the care of Mr. Greene of my former work [the first part of *Rights of Man*], have come safe to your hands."

THOMAS PAINE, 1737–1809. *Rights of man: being an answer to Mr. Burke's attack on the French revolution.* Philadelphia: Re-printed by S. H. Smith, 1791. This second Philadelphia edition is from the library of George Washington.

GEORGE WASHINGTON, 1732–1799. Autograph letter signed, dated Mount Vernon, 20 May 1792, to James Madison. 6 p. Washington expressed a desire to retire from the Presidency at the end of his first term and in this letter to Madison, then a Representative from Virginia, he asks Madison to write a valedictory address to the public for him and outlines what he would like to have incorporated in it. "I take the liberty at my departure from civil, as I formerly did at my military exit, to invoke a continuation of the blessings of Providence upon it [my country], and upon all those who are the supporters of its interests, and the promoters of harmony, order & good government." Circumstances forced Washington to remain in office for another term and the "Farewell Address" was not delivered until September 1796.

JOHN ADAMS, 1735–1826. Autograph letter signed, dated Quincy, 21 June 1811, addressed to Dr. Benjamin Rush, discussing his family and mutual friends, and the "angry, turbulent Stormy Science of Politicks." 4 p. The sec-

Mount Vernon May 20.th 1792.

My dear Sir,

As there is a possibility if not a probability, that I shall not see you on your return home; — or, if I should see you, that it may be on the Road and under circumstances which will prevent my speaking to you on the subject we last conversed upon; I take the liberty of committing to paper the following thoughts, & requests.

I have not been unmindful of the sentiments expressed by you in the conversations just alluded to: — on the contrary I have again, and again revolved them, with thoughtful anxiety; but without being able to dispose my mind to a longer continuation in the Office I have now the honor to hold. — I therefore still look forward to the fulfilment of my fondest and most ardent wishes to spend the remainder of my days (which I can not expect will be many) in ease & tranquility.

Nothing short of conviction that my dereliction of the Chair of Government (if it should be the desire of the people to continue me in it) would involve the Country in serious disputes respecting the chief Magistrate, & the dis agreeable consequences which might result there from in the floating, ~~and~~ divided opinions

which

WASHINGTON   Autograph Letter to Madison   1792

ond President of the United States writes of George Washington that "if he was not the greatest President he was the best actor of Presidency we have ever had." He is more critical of Thomas Jefferson: "The Declaration of Independence I always considered as a Theatrical Show. Jefferson ran away with all the Stage Effect of that: i.e. all the Glory of it."

Lent by the Heineman Foundation.

JOHN QUINCY ADAMS, 1767–1848. Autograph letter signed, The Hague, 11 February 1797, addressed to President Washington, praising the "Farewell Address" of the retiring President and thanking him for the public offices he has conferred on the writer. 2 p. The future sixth President of the United States, at this time Minister to The Netherlands, writes, ". . . as one of the People of the United States, I received your address to them dated on the 17th of September last. I fervently pray that they may not only impress all its admonitions upon their hearts, but that it may serve as the foundation upon which the whole system of their future policy may rise . . . I shall always consider my personal obligations to you among the strongest motives to animate my Industry and invigorate my exertions in the service of my Country."

Lent by the Heineman Foundation.

ALEXANDER HAMILTON, 1757–1804. Autograph letter signed, dated [Philadelphia] 6 May 1793, addressed to Robert Morris. 1 p. A letter of introduction for William Winstanley, "a Young Gentleman from England, who has lately turned his attention to Landscape painting." President Washington bought some of Winstanley's Hudson River landscapes, and also some landscapes of the Potomac in the area of the newly created Federal City. In 1795 Winstanley settled in New York City where he became a prominent portrait painter.

THOMAS JEFFERSON, 1743–1826. Two autograph letters signed, dated Lake Champlain, New York, and Bennington, Vermont, May and June 1791, ad-

My dear Martha   Lake George, Sun[day] M[ay]

I wrote to Maria yesterday, while
sailing on Lake George, & the same kind
of pleasure is afforded me to day to write to
you. Lake George is without comparison
the most beautiful water I ever saw; formed
by a contour of mountains into a basin ...
miles long, and from 2 to 4 miles broad,
finely interspersed with islands, its water
... as crystal & the mountain sides
covered with rich groves of Thuya, silver fir,
white pine, ... and paper birch down to
the water edge, here and there ...
... to chequer the scene & save it from
monotony. an abundance of speckled trout,
... salmon trout, bass, and other fish with
which it is stored, have added to our
other amusements. the sport ... when

Bennington in Vermont June 5. 1791.
Dear Sir

Mr Madison & myself are so far on
the tour we had projected. we have visited
in the course of it the principal scenes of
Burgoyne's misfortunes, to wit the ground
at Stillwater where the action of that name
was fought, and particularly the breast-
works which cost so much blood to both
parties, the encampments at Saratoga &
ground where the British piled their arms,
& the field of the battle of Bennington about 9
miles from this place. we have also visited
forts William Henry & George, Ticonderoga,
Crown point, &c. which have been scenes of blood
from a very early part of our history. we were
more pleased however with the botanical ...

JEFFERSON   Letters on Birch Bark   1791

By the President of the United States of America,
A Proclamation:

Whereas a certain Treaty and two several Conventions between the United States of America and the French Republic were concluded and signed by the Plenipotentiaries of the United States and the French Republic, duly and respectively authorised for that purpose, which Treaty and Conventions are, word for word, as follows: viz:

Treaty between the United States of America & the French Republic:

The President of the United States of America, and the First Consul of the French Republic, in the name of the French people, desiring to remove all source of misunderstanding relative to objects of discussion mentioned in the second and fifth articles of the convention of the 8th vendemiaire an. 9. (30th September, 1800,) relative to the rights claimed by the United States, in virtue of the Treaty concluded at Madrid the 27th of October 1795, between his Catholic Majesty and the said United States, and willing to strengthen the union and friendship which at the time of the said Convention was happily re-established between the two nations, have respectively named their Plenipotentiaries, to wit, the President of the United States of America, by and with the advice and consent of the Senate of the said States, Robert R Livingston, Minister Plenipotentiary of the United States, and James Monroe, Minister Plenipotentiary and Envoy Extraordinary of the said States, near the Government of the French Republic; and the first Consul, in the name of

JEFFERSON Proclamation of the Louisiana Purchase 1803

dressed to his daughter Martha (Mrs. Thomas M. Randolph) and his son-in-law. 9 p. Both letters are written on birch bark. The future President describes the beauties of New York State—although he still prefers Virginia—and comments on the battlefield at Bennington. At the end of the earlier letter Jefferson adds, "From this distance I can have little domestic to write to you about. I must always repeat how much I love you. Kiss the little Anne for me. I hope she grows lustily, enjoys good health, and will make us all, and long, happy as the centre of our common love."

THOMAS JEFFERSON, 1743–1826. By the President of the United States of America, A Proclamation, Whereas a certain Treaty and two several conventions between the United States of America and the French Republic were concluded. Manuscript document signed by President Jefferson and counter-signed by James Madison as Secretary of State. City of Washington, 1803. 18 p. With the Large Seal of the United States. This document is the original proclamation of the Louisiana Purchase. It begins with the complete text of the treaty negotiated in Paris, 30 April 1803, and contains an account of its ratification in Washington, the 21st "of this present month of October." This is a document of greatest importance in American history. Upon this proclamation the size of the United States more than doubled. At about four cents an acre, the purchase added nearly a million square miles.

Lent by Mrs. Charles W. Engelhard.

JEAN ANTOINE HOUDON, 1741–1828. Bust of Benjamin Franklin. Stucco (composition plaster). Signed: Houdon. French, c. 1779. First shown in the Paris Salon of 1779.

Lent by Mrs. Charles W. Engelhard.

JEAN ANTOINE HOUDON, 1741–1828. Life-mask of George Washington. Plaster. Unsigned. French, 1785. Made at Mount Vernon in preparation for the statue of Washington now in the rotunda of the State Capitol in Richmond.

JEAN ANTOINE HOUDON   Life-Mask of Washington   1785

Soldiers and Sailors

The trial of William Weems [and seven others] Soldiers in his Majesty's 29th Regiment of Foot, for the murder of Crispus Attucks [and four others] on Monday-evening, the 5th of March, 1770. . . . Boston: J. Fleeming, 1770. The Boston Massacre trial is one of the most famous in American history. There was much public feeling against the soldiers and they were defended by Josiah Quincy and John Adams, leaders of the cause of the Colonials. But the trial was a fair and impartial one; six of the soldiers were acquitted and the other two charged with manslaughter and burned in the hand.

New York Sons of Liberty. Manuscript muster roll, with the signatures of 104 citizens who organized against the oppressive measures of the British government. [New York, n.d.]. 1 p. The Sons of Liberty were members of secret organizations which sprang up during the summer of 1765 to oppose the Stamp Act. These groups occasionally resorted to intimidation and violence to harrass the British. The subscribers agreed, "We will provide ourselves, with a good Firelock, Bayonet, Cutlass, and a Cartouche-Box, . . . and that we shall meet . . . to learn the Manual and other Exercises and to perfect ourselves in the Military Art."

Paul Revere, 1735–1818. Autograph document signed, dated [Boston] 3 April 1795. 1 p. The celebrated silversmith and engraver, whose ride to warn the people of Lexington and Concord was immortalized in Longfellow's poem, wrote out this receipt for mending a plated terret with silver ferril for Thomas K. Jones, merchant and financier of Boston.

NEW YORK SONS OF LIBERTY   Manuscript Muster Roll

THE OLD NORTH BRIDGE. A piece of wood from the Old North Bridge of 1775, "the rude bridge that arched the flood," found in the river in Concord, Massachusetts, when the bridge was restored in 1956.

Gift of the Selectmen of Concord.

RICHARD MONTGOMERY, 1738–1775. Autograph letter signed, dated "Holland House" [near Quebec, c. 31 December 1775], addressed to Sir Guy Carleton. Probably the last letter written by the American general to the leader of the British forces in Quebec. He calls on Carleton to surrender during the difficult winter siege. "If you possess any share of humanity you will not sacrifice the Lives & properties of so many innocent people to a vain punctilio." Carleton refused and Montgomery was killed in the assault on Quebec that followed.

SAMUEL MATHER, 1706–1785. Autograph letter signed, dated Boston, 8 July 1776, addressed to "My dear Child" (a relative). 1 p. The son of Cotton Mather and Rector of Old North Church writes of the sudden death of Cousin Sally, who died "as Dr. Rand thinks of a proper Apoplexy." Paul Revere's signal lanterns were hung in the belfry arch of Old North Church; he married his second wife, Rachel Walker, in the church in 1773. This letter is dated four days after the signing of the Declaration of Independence.

Purchased as the gift of John P. Morgan, II.

MASSACHUSETTS-BAY. HOUSE OF REPRESENTATIVES. Printed broadside resolution, dated 20 January 1777, asking for blankets for the army, with a detailed list of towns and their quotas. "Resolved, That there be Five Thousand Blankets levied on the several Towns and Plantations in this State, in the several Proportions as expressed in this Schedule."

ARTICLES OF CONVENTION BETWEEN LT. GEN. BURGOYNE & MAJR. G
GATES. Manuscript signed by Burgoyne. 1 p. In 1777 the British troops at-
tempted to isolate New England by occupying the Hudson valley. General
Burgoyne, marching down from Canada, took Ticonderoga on 6 July, but
Generals Howe, from New York, and St. Leger, from Oswego, did not advance to meet him according to plan. Burgoyne's forces were severely defeated
by the Continentals led by General Benedict Arnold on 7 October, and the
British retreated. They were surrounded, however, at Saratoga by the forces
of General Gates. Burgoyne opened surrender negotiations on 14 October and
on the 16th sent these terms to Gates, who accepted them almost without
modification. Burgoyne insisted that the agreement must not be called a
capitulation, but a "Convention"—although his army was lost, his feelings
were spared. Gates's willingness to yield on so many points was, as Burgoyne
suspected, prompted by news of the army of General Clinton moving up from
New York. This is an original manuscript of the terms of a great American
victory—the turning point of the Revolution. Two other contemporary copies
are known.

WALTER BRYANT, JR. "Burguoyne's Defeat." Autograph manuscript, dated
November 1777. 2 p. This rustic ballad celebrates the downfall of the proud
and confident general in rhymed couplets that would have caused "Gentleman
Johnny" to wince on either military or literary grounds—for Burgoyne
achieved considerable success as a dramatist both before and after the American Revolution. The author appears to have been a soldier from Newmarket,
New Hampshire, who participated in the Battle of Saratoga but is otherwise
unknown to fame.

> "Thus swel'd old John & then he strode
> Athwart the Lane & down the road
> To dye the Reeds on Hudson's Shore
> With purling Streams of human Gore."

Gift of Laurens Morgan Hamilton.

Articles of Convention between L't Gen Burgoyne & Maj'r G'l Gates —

The Troops under L't G' Burgoyne are to march out of their Camp with the Honors of War — and the Artillery of the Intrenchments to the Verge of the River, where the old Fort Stood. Where the Arms & Artillery are to be left — the Arms to be Piled by Word of command from their own Officers

{ 2 }

A free Passage to be granted to the Army under L't G' Burgoyne to Great Brittain — upon condition of not Serving again in ... during the present contest — & the Port of Boston be assigned ... the entry of Transports to receive the Troops when ever Gene... shall so order ——— { 3 }

Should any Cartel ... the plan ... — by which the Army under L't G' ... or any part of it may be exchanged the foregoing Article Void as far as such Exchange shall be made

{ 4 }

The Army under L't G' B. to march to Massa Bay by the easiest, most expeditious & convenient Rout & to be quartered in — Near or as convenient as possible to Boston that the March of the Troops may not be delay'd when Transports shall arrive to receive them

{ 5 }

The Troops to be Supplied on the March & during their stay in ... with Provisions by G'l Gates' Order — at the same Rate of Rations as the Troops of his own Army & if Possible the Officers Horses & Cattle are to be Supplied with Forrage at the usual Rates —

{ 6 }

All Officers to Retain their Carriages — Bat Horses — & other Cattle & no Baggage to be molested or Searched — L't G' B. giving his Honor there are no Publick Stores Secreted therein — Maj' G' Gates w... of course take the necessary Measures for the due Performance of this Article — Sh'd any Carriages be wanting during the ... for the transportation of Officers Baggage — they are if Pos... to be Supplied by the Country at the usual Rates —

{ 7 }

Upon the March & during the time the army shall ... in ... in the Massa Bay — the Officers are not ... far as ... will admit to be Seperated from their ... The Officers are to be quartered according to their Rank & a... not to be hindred from assembling their Men for Role Calling & other purposes of Regularity —

{ 8 }

All Corps whatever of L't G' Burgoynes Army, whether composed of Sailors — Batteau men — Artificers, Drivers, Ind. Companies & followers of the Army of whatever Country — Shall be included in the fullest Sense & utmost Extent of the above Articles & comprehended in every Respect as Brittish Subjects ——

THE ARTICLES OF CONVENTION AT SARATOGA 1777

MARQUIS DE LA FAYETTE, 1757–1834. Autograph letter signed, dated Bethlehem, 14 October 1777, addressed to General Washington. 1 p. On 13 September 1777, La Fayette was wounded in the leg at the battle of Brandywine and was taken to Bethlehem, Pennsylvania, to recover. From there he wrote this remarkable letter to Washington, praising Generals Conway and De Kalb and asking for the command of a division. He did not realize that at that moment a group of officers, including Conway, was plotting to replace Washington by General Gates—the Conway Cabal. La Fayette addressed Washington "with all the confidence of a son, of a friend, as you favoured me with those two so precious titles."

CALEB JONES. *Orderly book.* Headquarters, Haddenfield, New Jersey, 18 June 1778, to Headquarters, Flushing, L.I., 12 October 1778. 167 p. The orderly book kept by Captain Jones of the Maryland Loyalists is a first-hand source for the day-by-day history of a British regiment during the Revolution. There are accounts of troop movements, provisions, daily orders, and courts-martial. Punishments were severe. "Prisioners Tryed by the Genl. Court Martial of which Lieut Cole Abercromby was President. John Monk Waggoner in the Qr. Mr. Genls. Department Tryed for Stealing Severrall picies of Broad Cloath Blanketts & when posted to take cear of said articles is Found Guilty and Sentenced to Receive 1000 Lashes. John Connolly Private Soldier in the 64th Battn Tryed for having Disserted from said Regt. is found Guilty and Sentenced to receve 1000 Lashes. John Morgan Sergt. of Genl. Paine is Tryed for Plundering is found Not Guilty and Therefore Acquited."

BARON FRIEDRICH VON STEUBEN, 1730–1794. Letter signed, dated White Plains, 1 September 1778, to Henry Laurens, President of Congress. 2 p. The celebrated Prussian soldier reported to General Washington at Valley Forge in February 1778 and undertook the training of the army. Within a few months the success of drills he gave to a model company spread throughout the army—a most remarkable achievement in rapid military training. In this letter he reports the critical situation of the troops in Rhode Island. "These news have determined Genl Washington to desire me to stay here this night in Expectation of an Express."

JOHN PAUL JONES, 1747–1792. Letter signed, dated Amsterdam, 13 October 1779, addressed to Robert Morris. 4 p. The battle on 23 September 1779 between the American ship, the *Bon Homme Richard*, commanded by Captain John Paul Jones, and the British ship, *Serapis*, was a famous victory for the United States. In this remarkable letter to Morris written by a secretary but signed by Jones three weeks after the battle he describes the action at sea in detail. He concludes, "At last the Enemy Struck the English Flagg—but the Victory was too dear."

MASSACHUSETTS-BAY. COUNCIL-CHAMBER. 30 June 1780. 1 p. A printed broadside calling for enlistments and reenlistments in the Colonial Army issued at the request of General Washington. This was a difficult time and men were badly needed. One other copy of this broadside is recorded. ". . . all persons who are fired with love of Freedom, and scorn to be Slaves, be and hereby are called upon to exert themselves, in the most speedy and expeditious manner, to compleat their respective Quotas." "If we mean to be FREE, this is the moment to exert ourselves."

COMTE DE ROCHAMBEAU, 1725–1807. Letter signed and partly in his autograph, dated Newport, 16 July 1780, addressed to the Marquis de La Fayette. 3 p. The French fleet arrived at Newport in July 1780 and La Fayette met the commander, the Comte de Rochambeau, on 25 July. On his way to Rhode Island this letter reached him. Rochambeau looks forward to the meeting and remarks that one hour of conversation can accomplish more than volumes of correspondence. The closing sentence reads in translation, "I embrace you, my dear Marquis, most heartily, and don't make me any more compliments, I beg of you."

JOHN PAUL JONES   Gouache Portrait

[JOHN ANDRÉ], 1751–1780. Autograph letter signed, dated New York, 7 September 1780, addressed to Colonel Sheldon. 3 p. Major André, using the name of "John Anderson," represented the British in negotiations with Benedict Arnold for the surrender of West Point. He was captured on 23 September and the whole treason was exposed. A court-martial of fourteen general officers found André guilty of spying and he was executed on 2 October. This letter written on 7 September to Colonel Sheldon was intended to be placed in Arnold's hands. It is signed "John Anderson" and asks permission for a meeting with "a friend near your Outposts."

BENEDICT ARNOLD, 1741–1801. Autograph letter signed, dated Robinson's House, 23 August 1780, addressed to Major General Greene. 1 p. The Revolutionary patriot and traitor had already begun his secret negotiations with General Clinton for the betrayal of West Point at the time this letter was written. He complains at great length about the inactivity of Congress and its failure to support the army. Arnold's disturbances with civil authorities in Pennsylvania led Congress to order a court-martial for him; Congress had also promoted five generals over his head. "Congress could not have taken more effectual measures to derange, and throw several departments into Confusion than has been pursued for sometime past, the Consequences of which I am afraid will be severely felt by the Army, and may be attended with fatal Consequences to the Public."

JOSEPH EGGLESTON, 1754–1811. Autograph letter signed, dated Hackinsack, 28 September 1780, addressed to an unidentified recipient. 2 p. Eggleston was a member of Congress from Virginia and a Revolutionary officer. Less than a week after the discovery of Benedict Arnold's treasonable plot to betray West Point, the American Gibraltar, Eggleston wrote this detailed letter outlining all the details of the conspiracy as he knew them. He describes the activities of both Arnold and Major André, including Arnold's escape and André's capture. ". . . all the influence of Arnold himself, prevailed, and he was placed in that important fortress. Here he had full leisure and opportunity to pursue his hellish plan which was blasted only a day before its intended execution by the merest chain of accidents, and which plainly point us out as under the peculiar direction of Providence."

CHARLES CORNWALLIS, 2D EARL, 1738–1805. Manuscript proclamation, dated Head Quarters [North Carolina], 8 March 1781, offering amnesty to the "rebels." 1 p. The "rebels" saw no reason to surrender in North Carolina when the Redcoats were obviously on the run; the surrender at Yorktown was not far in the future. Although there are drafts of this proclamation in the Cornwallis Papers in the Public Record Office, this appears to be the official copy— the one which was proclaimed. "Whereas it has been represented to me that many Persons in this Province, who have taken a Share in this unnatural Rebellion . . . are sincerely desirous of returning to their duty and Allegiance. . . ."
Gift of the estate of Hall Park McCullough.

CHARLES CORNWALLIS, 2D EARL, 1738–1805. Letter signed, dated York, Virginia, 17 October 1781, addressed to General Washington. 1 p. This is the letter which Lord Cornwallis sent to General Washington asking for surrender terms. It is one of the great letters of American history. "I propose a Cessation of Hostilities for Twenty four hours, and that two Officers may be appointed by each side to meet at Mr. Moore's house to settle terms for the surrender of the posts of York & Gloucester."

GEORGE WASHINGTON, 1732–1799. Letter (in the hand of William S. Smith) signed, dated Head Quarters near York, 24 October 1781, addressed to Major General Nathaniel Greene. 2 p. General Washington gives an account of the events leading to the surrender of Cornwallis. "This proposition the first that passed between us, led to a Corespondence which terminated in a definitive Capitulation which was agreed to and signed the 19th. In which His Lordship surrenders himself and Troops prisoners of War to the American Army;

York, Virginia 17th Octr. 1781

Sir

I propose a Cessation of Hostilities
for Twenty four hours, and that two Officers may
be appointed by each side to meet at Mr. Moore's
house to settle terms for the surrender of the
posts of York & Gloucester. I have the honour
to be

Sir

Your most obedient &
most humble Servant

Cornwallis

His Excellency
General Washington
&c. &c. &c.

LORD CORNWALLIS   Letter to General Washington   1781

march'd out with Colours Cased, & drums beating a British march, to a post in front of their lines, where their Arms were grounded; the public Stores, Arms, Artillery, Military Chest, &c. delivered to the American Army." Accompanied by a manuscript draft of the surrender terms at Yorktown drawn up in an unidentified hand.

REUBEN SANDERSON, 1754 – c. 1825. Autograph diary with entries dated from 1775 to 1815. 138 p. The diary includes Sanderson's experiences in the Revolutionary War in which he served as a Lieutenant; there is a good account of the march to and siege of Yorktown. He was also a poet. A long battle poem begins:

> "Whilst in peacefull Quarters lying
> We indulge the glas till late
> Far remot the thoughts of dying
> Hear my frinds the Soldiers fate
> From the summer sun hot gleaming
> Whear the dusty clouds arise
> To the plains where hearos screaming
> Shout and dying groons arise—"

TADEUSZ KOSCIUSZKO, 1746–1817. Autograph letter signed [docketed received 14 April 1798], addressed to Thomas Jefferson. 1 p. The Polish patriot Kosciuszko served with distinction throughout the war and was a great aid to the American cause. He wrote this appeal to Jefferson at the conclusion of a visit to the United States in 1798 during which he had been honored with gifts of money and a grant of land in Ohio. ". . . do not forget that jam under your protection, and you only my resource in this Country." Kosciuszko continued to fight for the liberation of Poland. After his death his American lands were sold and the funds used to found the Colored School at Newark, New Jersey, one of the first educational institutions for black children in America.

THE UNION

THE DECLARATION OF INDEPENDENCE. *In Congress, 4 July 1776, A Declaration.* Philadelphia: John Dunlap, 1776. Sometime on the night of 4 July or the morning of the next day this first printing of the *Declaration of Independence* came off the press and was rapidly dispatched to officials throughout the Colonies to be reprinted in broadside form and in newspapers. It is the embodiment of a great historical event and is the heart of our Bicentennial celebrations. Fifteen copies of this printing have survived.

Lent anonymously.

THE GREAT SEAL OF THE STATE OF NEW YORK. The Great Seal and Privy Seal were created by statute in 1778 and the Great Seal was used in the form shown here until 1798. The upper side shows the sun rising from behind mountains, with "The Great Seal of the State of New York" written around the margin. The document to which the Great Seal is affixed is signed by Governor George Clinton (the second Governor of this name) and certifies Gilbert Livingston as a Master in the Court of Chancery. It is dated 13 January 1784 from New York City; Albany did not become the capital of New York State until 1797. Clinton served seven terms as Governor and was twice elected Vice-President of the United States.

With a seal of the Province of New York showing the Indians doing homage to King George III. (Lent by Charles Ryskamp.)

[THOMAS JEFFERSON], 1743–1826. *Notes on the state of Virginia.* [Paris: Phillipe Denis Pierres, 1785]. Jefferson's book about his native state was first published in France and widely reprinted there and in England. He tried to keep the book from the eyes of his fellow Virginians because of his outspoken and bitter remarks on slavery. It is rich in information about all aspects of life in Virginia. This copy was presented by Jefferson to the Comte de Rochambeau, "whose services to the American union in general entitle him to homage of all its citizens."

SAMUEL HUNTINGTON, 1731–1796. Manuscript proclamation. Norwich, Connecticut, 26 February 1787. 2 p. The rebellion led mainly by Daniel Shays of Massachusetts in 1786 and 1787 was the result of the failure of the Massachusetts legislature to do anything for the plight of debt-ridden farmers. In December 1786, Shays led a raiding party on the Springfield arsenal. The rebels were hunted down and eventually pardoned, but the rebellion made the States of the Confederation aware that they were powerless to protect themselves from invasion or domestic violence. Governor Bowdoin of Massachusetts thought that Shays would flee to Connecticut and asked Governor Huntington to issue this proclamation. Huntington was a Signer of the Declaration of Independence and President of the Continental Congress.

THE FEDERALIST: A COLLECTION OF ESSAYS, WRITTEN IN FAVOUR OF THE NEW CONSTITUTION, AS AGREED UPON BY THE FEDERAL CONVENTION, SEPTEMBER 17, 1787. New-York: J. and A. M'Lean, 1788. The eighty-five essays of *The Federalist* were originally published in the form of letters to three New York newspapers, with the purpose of persuading voters in New York State to accept the Constitution. They were written by John Jay (5), James Madison (14), Alexander Hamilton (63), and Madison and Hamilton together (3); they were edited by Hamilton and published in these two volumes. This first edition of the most influential political work is from the library of George Washington.

Lent by H. Bradley Martin.

U. S. CONSTITUTION. [Philadelphia, 6 August 1787]. The first draft of the report of the committee of the Federal Convention on the Constitution. It was printed for the use of members in an edition of not more than sixty copies, on one side of seven leaves. This copy was owned and is heavily annotated by Abraham Baldwin, a member of the Continental Congress, and later Representative and Senator from Georgia. Baldwin was influential in framing the compromise system of representation, by states in the Senate and by population in the House. A second draft was published 12 September; copies of both drafts are extremely rare and highly prized, especially when annotated.

U.S. CONSTITUTION. [Newport: Peter Edes, 1790]. Rhode Island was the last of the states to ratify the Constitution on 29 May 1790, nearly a year after the Constitution had been declared in effect. This is the first edition printed in that state. With it is the *Ratification of the Constitution of the United States by the Convention of the State of Rhode-Island and Providence-Plantations*, also printed by Peter Edes. The *Constitution* and *Ratification* may have been printed together on one large sheet and separated later for convenience in use.

U.S. CONSTITUTION. Manuscript proposal of the eleventh amendment to the Constitution. Philadelphia, 1793. 1 p. "The judicial power of the United States shall not be construed to extend to any suit in law or equity, commenced or prosecuted against one of the United States by Citizens of another State or by Citizens or Subjects of any foreign State." The document is signed by John Adams, Vice-President, Frederick Augustus Muhlenberg, Speaker of the House, and John Beckley and Samuel A. Otis, clerks. This, the first amendment after the Bill of Rights, was ratified in 1798.

JAMES MADISON, 1751–1836. Autograph letter signed, dated [New York] 29 January 1789, addressed to Colonel Thompson. 8 p. This long letter, written while Madison was a Representative in Congress, deals entirely with the term "direct taxes" as used in the Constitution and with the understanding of the people of the United States concerning that term when they adopted the Constitution. Over a century later, in 1895, this letter was published in *The Nation*, at the time that the U.S. Supreme Court declared the Income Tax Law of 1894 to be unconstitutional because it was a direct tax, and provoked much comment. Madison believed that the Constitution authorized direct taxation and, as we all know, we now have the Sixteenth Amendment to implement this belief.

Printed by
The Stinehour Press